Magna Carta
Text and Commentary

MAGNA CARTA

Text and Commentary
Revised Edition

A. E. DICK HOWARD
University of Virginia

University Press of Virginia
Charlottesville and London

THE UNIVERSITY PRESS OF VIRGINIA
© 1964, 1998 by the Rector and Visitors of the University of Virginia
All rights reserved. First edition 1964
Revised edition 1998
Printed in the United States of America

First published 1998

Front cover: This woodcut of King John first appeared in John Rastell's
The Pastime of People (1529).

The paper used in this publication meets the minimum requirements of
the American National Standard for Information Sciences—Permanence of
Paper for Printed Library Materials, ANSI Z39.48-1984.

Library of Congress Cataloging-in-Publication Data

Howard, A. E. Dick.
     Magna carta : text and commentary / A. E. Dick Howard. — Rev. ed.
          p. cm.
     Includes bibliographical references.
     ISBN 0-8139-0121-9 (pbk. : alk. paper)
     1. Magna Carta. 2. Constitutional history—Great Britain.
     I. Magna Carta. II. Title.
     KD3946.H69   1997
     342.42'029—dc21
                                                           97-35659
                                                           CIP

FOREWORD

At the dawn of the third millennium, historians and constitutionalists the world over will look back and seek to identify the crucial turning points in the long struggle to establish freedom under the law. There will no doubt be many candidates, and different experts will have their own favourites. But few could deny a place of honour to the Great Charter sealed by King John "in the meadow which is called Runnymede, between Windsor and Staines," on June 15, 1215. The Charter was to transform constitutional thinking not only in the land of its birth but also in the United States, Canada, India, and vast areas of the world which learned from their example. The charter did not, of course, spring fully formed into new life. The rebellious barons, like all wise revolutionaries, drew on earlier precedents, in particular the coronation charters of John's Angevin predecessors. Nor were the barons engaged in an exercise in political philosophy: their concerns were down-to-earth and far from altruistic. But from this clash between a hard, obstinate King and tough, self-interested barons there emerged, improbably, principles which have resounded down the centuries and retain their resonance today.

No free man shall be taken, imprisoned, disseised, outlawed, banished, or in any way destroyed, nor will We proceed against or prosecute him, except by the lawful judgment of his peers and by the law of the land.

To no one will We sell, to none will We deny or delay, right or justice.

Even on a literal reading, these provisions forbid the exercise of arbitrary, unaccountable power. As developed by ingenious lawyers on both sides of the Atlantic, they have proved the most powerful obstacle to tyranny the world has ever seen.

This publication, in a revised edition, of Professor A. E. Dick Howard's *Magna Carta: Text and Commentary* is very greatly to be welcomed. He is a leading authority on many areas of constitutionalism. His knowledge is profound. His insights are illuminating. A new generation of readers will, I hope, experience the excitement of examining those events, now nearly 800 years ago, which yet remain the foundation of our shared constitutional faith.

THE RT HON LORD BINGHAM OF CORNHILL
Lord Chief Justice of England

Royal Courts of Justice
Strand, London WC2, February 1997

CONTENTS

FOREWORD by Lord Bingham of Cornhill   v

COMMENTARY   1

King John and the Barons   3

The Provisions of Magna Carta   8

    FEUDAL RELATIONSHIPS   9

    COURTS AND THE ADMINISTRATION OF JUSTICE   12

    ABUSES OF LOCAL OFFICIALS   16

    CORRECTION OF THE KING'S PAST WRONGS   18

    FOREST CLAUSES   18

    TOWNS AND TRADE   18

    DEBTS AND ESTATES   19

    CHURCH AND STATE   20

    SECURITY FOR THE KEEPING OF THE CHARTER   20

    GENERAL CLAUSES   21

Magna Carta's Influence   22

THE TEXT OF MAGNA CARTA   33

BIBLIOGRAPHICAL NOTE   55

COMMENTARY

KING JOHN AND THE BARONS

Few of the English barons who gathered at a meadow called Runnymede on June 15, 1215, were thinking whether their day's work would survive to be acclaimed, or even remembered, in future centuries. They were practical men, with specific grievances against their King. In May they had renounced all allegiance to the Crown, and now they were gathered to present their demands, in the form of articles, to King John for his seal. At the moment that seal was affixed, the course of history was changed. Much of what those rude, mostly unlettered, and generally selfish barons won for themselves that June day, they won for generations yet unborn.

Magna Carta might have died. Indeed, so little attention was paid to it in Tudor times that Shakespeare's *King*

John does not even mention the Charter. But the idea of freedom from arbitrary government which it planted took root to flourish in later ages. Such magic did the name "Magna Carta" come to have for free men that in the seventeenth century, when Englishmen were resisting the excesses of the Stuart kings, Sir Edward Coke said, "Magna Charta is such a Fellow, he will have no Sovereign," and the ideals of the Great Charter were carried ashore along with the first charter of the Virginia Company by the earliest settlers at Jamestown. When revolutionary fevers rose in the eighteenth century, American colonists were to invoke Magna Carta in defense of their liberties and, having secured their independence, were to write into their new Constitution a guarantee of "due process of law," an ideal traceable to Magna Carta's promise that none should be proceeded against save by the "law of the land."

The history of England after the Norman Conquest of 1066 is one of unconscious struggle forward from being an inconsequential island off the continent of Europe toward becoming a great nation that would send its men and language and laws around the world. William the Conqueror not only brought order, he also brought power—power which the barons, preferring to be petty monarchs themselves, often resisted. William, carefully importing into England the Norman customs that suited him, laid the foundation for a strong central government. In the next century Henry II, through energetic reforms such as reorganization of the courts to bring litigation into the royal courts (with the revenues coming to the Crown) instead of into the baronial courts, caused the central administration to attain even greater efficiency and the monarchy new levels of power.

In the reign of Henry, the exercise of royal power did not stir any great body of opinion against him, but already England was being increasingly exploited to support wars abroad. With the accession of Richard I, "the Lion-Hearted," in 1189, England began to feel more severely the weight of royal prerogative. The adventuresome and reckless Richard cared, not for affairs of state, but for war. Only twice before his accession at the age of thirty-two had he been in England, and as King he looked to England mostly as a source of revenues for his adventures abroad. During the ten years of his reign, during which he joined the Third Crusade to fight against Saladin's army in the Holy Land and carried on a sporadic war with Philip Augustus of France, Richard was in England only a few months altogether. Yet all the while his ministers were continually pressed by their master to extract still more taxes, levies, and contributions from Richard's subjects—including an enormous ransom required to effect Richard's release after he fell into the hands of Henry VI, the Holy Roman Emperor. The odium of these taxes bore not on Richard himself, who became a popular hero for his exploits abroad, but on his ministers, who often lined their own pockets while raising money for their master.

After Richard's death in 1199, his brother, John, continued Richard's heavy taxes, but as John was not an absentee king the discontent over royal taxations fell upon him personally. Soon other problems mounted. To begin with, John poured money and fruitless efforts into a war with the King of France, Philip Augustus, only to have enormous parts of the English King's French possessions—even Normandy itself, land of John's ancestors—fall into French hands. The barons had already shown their unwillingness to aid John in his wars with France, and the severance of Normandy, entailing the loss of the barons' Norman landholdings, made the barons turn their attention even more to English affairs, including their grievances against the King. Then John quarreled with the Pope, Innocent III, over the election of a new Archbishop of Canterbury; when the monks of Canterbury elected one candidate and John named another, Innocent III chose yet a third, Stephen Langton. John refused to recognize the Pope's appointment and thus precipitated a contest which saw the whole of England come under a papal interdict suspending church services and sacraments—a powerful weapon in an age of faith—and John himself excommunicated. Still John fought back, seizing church properties, until the Pope threatened to release the English people from their allegiance to the Crown. Finally John gave in, agreeing to accept Stephen Langton as Archbishop, to restore church property, to recall exiled churchmen, and to receive his kingdom as a fief from the Pope—altogether, a full surrender to the demands of Innocent III.

Thus, however ignominiously, John extricated himself from France and from his contest with the Pope. But he had yet to reckon with the rising grievances of his own people. The barons were increasingly bitter over the weight of taxation and feudal obligations, particularly exactions to support a French war in which many had no interest. Nor were grievances limited to the barons. Royal officials took, often without payment, lesser men's food, timber, horses, and carts. After the general eyre (a system of itinerant courts to hear pleas in the localities) was held in 1208, justice became more sporadic, despite John's attentions to the courts, with the result that abuses by John's officials often went unchecked. The towns, too, were complaining of heavy taxation, while the spoliation of the Church during John's quarrel with Rome bore heavily upon the poor of the realm, since the Church was the source of poor relief in that age. Even John's reconciliation with the Pope brought John new enemies—those who wanted to see the English Church free of domination from Rome.

The storm was gathering. In 1212 John had to call off a Welsh expedition because of warnings that his disaffected barons were on the verge of revolt. The next year John became enraged at the northern barons because many of them failed to support an expedition to France. He marched north, bent on vengeance, but relented on the plea of Archbishop Langton, who submitted that the barons should be punished only if tried in the King's courts and found guilty—a position prophetic of the guarantee of a trial according to the "law of the land" given two years later in chapter 39 of Magna Carta. By 1214, when John returned in total defeat from France, he found that discontent had ripened into active agreement among his opponents that the time was at hand for redress of their grievances. Meeting with the King at Bury St. Edmunds, the barons unequivocally refused to pay a scutage (a payment required in lieu of rendering personal military services to one's lord) demanded by John.

The barons agreed among themselves that, unless the King confirmed their liberties by charter, they would withdraw their allegiance, and they began preparations for war. In Easter week of 1215 they presented their demands, which were peremptorily refused by the explosive monarch: "Why do not the barons, with these unjust exactions, ask my kingdom?" In May the barons formally renounced their allegiance. John found his situation desperate. He sought to win over opponents in the Church by granting the Church freedom of election of vacant sees and to gain support in London by granting that city the right to annual election of its own mayor; both efforts failed.

As with many crises, events moved swiftly. The barons refused John's offer of arbitration–probably a delaying tactic on the part of the King–and marched on London. When that city opened its gates to the barons, John knew that he must come to terms. The capitulation came with John's message to the barons that he would "freely accede to the laws and liberties which they asked" if they would set a date and place to meet. The date they fixed was June 15, the place, Runnymede. The barons came prepared with a list of their demands, the Articles of the Barons. The King having agreed to the articles, they were then reduced to the form of a charter. With the affixing of the King's Great Seal on June 19, firm peace was reached. Although it was in the form of a 1225 reissue that the Charter became embodied in the statute books as part of the corpus of English law, the events of 1215 gave birth to the document which a later generation came to call "Magna Carta."

THE PROVISIONS OF MAGNA CARTA

The Charter to which John agreed is an intensely practical document. Rarely does its language sound of rhetoric. Far from being a philosophical tract dealing in lofty generalities, it is keyed to the problems at hand, spelling out one by one concrete remedies for actual abuses. Yet because the problems of the fair administration of justice, of the restraint of petty officials, of the relations between free men and their government—in short, of the quest for a rule of law—have a universality that transcends the specific grievances of the barons of Runnymede, this practical document became and remains today one of the great birthrights of men who love liberty.

As drawn in June 1215, the Charter was not carefully organized; often, related problems are dealt with in scattered parts of the document. Indeed, Magna Carta, unlike a modern statute or constitution, was not broken down into numbered or lettered parts. For convenience of reference, however, the 1215 Charter has been divided in later times into sixty-three traditional "chapters," a practice which we will follow in the text of the Charter that follows this commentary.

Many of the chapters of Magna Carta concern the intricacies of feudal relationships, problems which are of no concern in modern times. Certain chapters, however, raise issues as vital today—and, in many parts of the world, as unresolved—as they were in the thirteenth century. A brief inquiry into the Charter is made easier, and its interest to modern times made sharper, by grouping the chapters into several categories.

FEUDAL RELATIONSHIPS. In many ways Magna Carta is a kind of road map of English feudalism in the reign of King John. Feudalism was the way in which a society organized itself in medieval Europe, varying somewhat from one land to another. Great landowners—in England, the barons—held their lands in "fee" from the King. In return for their fiefs, they took an oath of allegiance (which the barons in May of 1215 renounced), promising to render the King so many knights, according to their landholdings, when war or internal disorder required a military force. Those who held lands in fee from the King in turn subinfeudated their lands to men of lesser rank, and so it went. Not only could the King demand military service ("knights' fees"), he also could demand special taxes or "aids," for example, ransoms to free the King if taken prisoner and aids for the knighting of the King's eldest son or the marriage of his eldest daughter. Moreover, he had such privileges as guardianship (with the estate's profits) of heirs who had not yet come of age and the right to choose husbands, at a price, for widows and daughters of deceased barons.

Not only did the King have these rights against the barons, they in turn enjoyed such rights against their tenants. One can readily imagine that such a system invited exploitation, and at least fifteen of the chapters of Magna Carta regulate abuses which had crept into feudal relationships at all levels. *Chapters 2 and 3* together put a ceiling on the "reliefs" to be paid by heirs claiming their inheritance and provide that heirs under age need pay no relief. *Chapters 4 and 5* protect heirs against rapacious or unworthy guardians by allowing a guardian to take only "reasonable" profits from the heir's lands, by requiring the guardian to forfeit his guardianship and to make amends when he wastes the heir's property, and by enjoining the guardian to keep and maintain the heir's houses and other properties with revenues from the estate and to turn over the lands properly stocked when the heir comes of age. The parallel might be noted between these thirteenth-century rules imposed for the benefit of the heir and the close watch that modern courts keep over guardians, who are required to account for their dealings with the property of their wards. *Chapter 37* also pertains to guardianships. *Chapter 6* deals with the marriage of heirs, *chapter 7* secures to a widow her dower rights (compare modern rights of dower), and *chapter 8* humanely declares, "No widow shall be compelled to marry so long as she has a mind to live without a husband...."

Chapter 12 limits aids to three kinds: to ransom the King's person, to knight the King's eldest son, and to marry the King's eldest daughter (limited, out of prudence, to one marriage for that daughter). Moreover, all of these aids must be "reasonable" in amount. Finally, chapter 12 provides that no other aid shall be levied save by "common counsel" of the kingdom, and *chapter 14* spells out how this common counsel shall be had: the summoning, with forty days' notice, of a council to meet on a fixed date at a fixed place. These chapters are of special interest because later generations have often declared that they stated the principle of "no taxation without representation." This puts the argument for the significance of chapters 12 and 14 in too strong and too modern a form. Nevertheless, it is not hard to see that in the notion that at least some kinds of exactions could not be had without consent there lay a ready example for those who in later ages sought ancient precedents for the claim of the right of a people to be taxed only with their consent.

Chapter 15 extends to all "free men" the assurance, given to the barons in chapter 12, that levies may be exacted from them only for the three specified kinds of aids and that those aids must be "reasonable." *Chapter 16* limits the service which must be performed for a "knight's fee." Other provisions in the Charter—*chapters 32, 43, and 46* —deal with the return of the lands of convicted felons to the lords of the fees, the holding of escheats, and the guardianship of abbeys.

COURTS AND THE ADMINISTRATION OF JUSTICE. Because the oppressions of the King and the unjust exactions of officials often went unredressed through failure to abide by legal procedures and the laws of the realm, Magna Carta pays special attention to the machinery of justice and carefully spells out where courts are to sit, what procedures shall be followed, and how punishments can be meted out. These chapters, above all others, have made Magna Carta a symbol to later ages and have contributed most significantly to Anglo-American concepts of justice. *Chapter 17* is of special interest. Prior to Magna Carta the courts followed the person of the King wherever he went. Persons seeking justice therefore had to undergo the expense, delay, and frustrations of pursuing the King in his constant movements about the countryside; indeed, one plaintiff followed the King through England and France for five years before his case could be heard. Chapter 17 was a great step toward a modern system of accessible and inexpensive justice, for it declared, "Common Pleas shall not follow Our Court, but shall be held in some certain place." The "certain place," while not named in the Charter, turned out to be Westminster, in London.

Chapter 18, like chapter 17, makes justice more convenient and accessible. Chapter 18 requires that trials concerning three named writs, novel disseisin, mort d'ancestor, and darrein presentment—all concerning rights in real property—must be held in the county where the property is situated. *Chapter 19* provides a means for completing the assizes if they cannot be concluded on the day called for in chapter 18. While the writs in question have long since ceased to be of interest to any but antiquarians, the principle enunciated in chapter 18 is still vital in Anglo-American notions of justice: that local issues should be tried locally. We place special value on the ideal of local trial in our criminal law; one of the guarantees given a criminal defendant by the Sixth Amendment to the American Constitution is that he shall be tried by an impartial jury "of the State and district wherein the crime shall have been committed."

That the punishment should fit the crime is the philosophy expressed in *chapter 20*. The chapter declares that a free man shall be amerced (fined) only "according to the measure" of his offense, whether it be trivial or serious. Moreover, chapter 20 requires that fines not be so heavy as to jeopardize a free man's ability to make a living; the same protection is extended to merchants, whose business is not to be ruined, and to villeins (serfs attached to the manors), whose "tillage" (crops and lands under cultivation) is to be saved. *Chapter 21* likewise says that earls and barons shall be fined "in proportion to the measure of the offense," and *chapter 22* protects clerks in holy orders in the same way. The feeling that every man, including a criminal, ought to receive his due, and that the criminal law ought not to be administered in a vindictive or unduly oppressive way, recurs again and again in the great libertarian documents of English and American history. One need only recall, by way of example, the declaration in the English Bill of Rights of 1689 that "excessive bail ought not to be required, nor excessive fines imposed; nor cruel and unusual punishments inflicted," and the almost identical language of Amendment Eight of the Constitution of the United States.

In its meaning for later ages, including our own, one chapter in Magna Carta stands out above all others: it is the famed *chapter 39*. It declares, "No free man shall be taken, imprisoned, disseised, outlawed, banished, or in any way destroyed, nor will We proceed against or prosecute him, except by the lawful judgment of his peers and by the law of the land." Blackstone, having spoken in his *Commentaries* of other parts of the Charter, observed that chapter 39 all by itself "would have merited the title that it bears, of the *great* charter . . . ." This was no exaggeration. Although overly ambitious claims have been made for chapter 39—for example, that "judgment of his peers" is to be identified with our system of trial by jury—the requirement that one be tried by the "law of the land" had enormous significance in the development of one of our most precious ideals: the rule of law, a government of laws and not of men. Chapter 39 has two aspects: that of substance and that of procedure. It realizes, to begin with, that sentence should not be executed upon a man unless there has first been a judgment that he is guilty of some offense which the law recognizes as an offense. But the chapter also requires that there must be more than the formality of a legal judgment; there must be a genuine trial, not a hollow mockery. This means that the trial must be before a competent tribunal that follows accepted procedures. Then, and only then, has the "law of the land" been satisfied.

In Magna Carta's "law of the land" we can find the early origins of the concept of "due process of law," one of the cornerstones of our jurisprudence. In fact, as early as 1354 the words "due process" were used in an English statute interpreting Magna Carta, and by the end of the fourteenth century "due process of law" and "law of the land" were interchangeable. The Fifth Amendment to the Constitution of the United States is talking about "law of the land" when it says that no person shall be deprived of "life, liberty, or property, without due process of law." So is the Fourteenth Amendment when it places the same restriction on the States. Although "due process" as used in the Fourteenth Amendment includes rights unknown in the thirteenth century—for example, a criminal defendant's right to counsel—the debt to Magna Carta's "law of the land" is unquestionable.

Chapter 40 states another great principle: that justice is not something to be sold to the highest bidder but should be available on impartial terms to men of all ranks. Chapter 40 states, "To no one will We sell, to none will We deny or delay, right or justice." This does not mean that litigants in the courts can expect to be charged no fees at all; it simply means that justice is not an article of trade, and its price is not to be determined according to what the market will bear. In King John's time chapter 40 served to eliminate at least the worst abuses; as a standard to guide the administration of justice in later centuries, its influence was great. If taken to mean that the courts should be open to rich and poor alike, it commends itself to modern times as well.

The ideal of a rule of law, binding even the King, is suggested by several other chapters. *Chapter 24* forbids sheriffs, constables, coroners, and other royal officials—who had earned reputations as local tyrants—to try lawsuits that ought to be heard in the royal courts. To make sure that, wherever cases are heard, justice will be done, John promises in *chapter 45* that he will appoint as justices, constables, sheriffs, and bailiffs only men who "know the law of the land and will keep it well." *Chapter 38* forbids a bailiff to put a man to trial upon his own unsupported accusation without producing credible witnesses. Another chapter limiting the King's arbitrary acts, though not dealing with the courts, is *chapter 23*, which makes the King end his illegal practice of increasing the obligations of villages and individuals to build bridges.

Other chapters relating to trials include *chapter 34*, which says that the writ praecipe shall not issue with respect to landholding if it ousts the jurisdiction of the baron's courts; apparently its purpose was to save the barons the trouble of appearing in the royal court to claim a case. *Chapter 36* provides that the writ of inquisition (a writ relating to trial by combat and not, as often supposed, to habeas corpus) shall be given gratis and not refused. *Chapter 54* says that no one shall be arrested or imprisoned on the appeal of a woman for the death of any person except her husband; this represented an effort to end what was thought to be the unfair advantage enjoyed by women litigants, who could appoint a champion to fight for them in the trial by combat, while the unfortunate accused man had to do his own fighting.

ABUSES OF LOCAL OFFICIALS. "Power tends to corrupt," Lord Acton once said, and the petty officials of thirteenth-century England were not immune from this tendency. In addition to those chapters, mentioned earlier, dealing with the administration of justice, Magna Carta contains several chapters aimed at abuses imposed on the people by local officials. *Chapter 25,* aimed at the sheriffs, says that rents charged the counties and their subdivisions must remain at the ancient levels and not be increased. Four provisions, *chapters 28, 29, 30, and 31,* are of special interest. These are the chapters which protect men from arbitrary seizure of their property without the payment of compensation. At the time of Magna Carta, the King had various rights of "purveyance," that is, the right to appropriate, upon payment of compensation, necessaries for the use of his household, which was often on the move from place to place. But the practice was open to great abuses. Frequently, the price paid by unscrupulous royal officials was grossly inadequate (officials might even make an inside profit by charging the King more than had been paid), or payment might be long delayed.

Although Magna Carta did not abolish or even restrict the right of the Crown to requisition provisions, it did regulate the abuses practiced by royal officials and did so in terms which we in modern times find familiar. Chapter 28 says that no official shall take corn or other chattels from any man without immediate payment unless the seller voluntarily allows payment to be postponed. Chapter 29 deals with abuses attending the providing of castle guards. Chapter 30 forbids horses or carts to be requisitioned without the owner's consent, and chapter 31 requires consent before wood can be taken. The Constitution of the United States strikes a comparable balance between the needs of the state and the rights of private property; it declares, in the Fifth Amendment, not that no property may ever be taken by the Federal Government, but rather that "just compensation" must always be paid when private property is taken for "public use." The Fourteenth Amendment has long been construed to place the same requirement on the States.

CORRECTION OF THE KING'S PAST WRONGS. A number of the chapters of Magna Carta essay to redress wrongs done during the struggle between the King and the barons. *Chapters 49, 58, and 59* require the return of English, Welsh, and Scottish hostages. *Chapters 52, 56, and 57* state that lands, castles, liberties, or rights unlawfully taken shall be restored, and *chapter 55* requires the remission of fines unjustly exacted. Chapter 52 is qualified by a respite given the King if he went on the Crusades; a like respite as to several other promises made by the King is given in *chapter 53*. By *chapter 62* King John fully pardons all "ill-will, wrath, and malice" which has risen between himself and his subjects. *Chapter 51* declares that all mercenaries shall be expelled from the kingdom, and *chapter 50* names specific Poitevins, obnoxious to the barons, who may not hold any office in England.

FOREST CLAUSES. Royal forests were districts set aside by the King for sport and hunting. Within these districts the English common law was supplemented by a much stricter, and harsher, "forest law." The existence of these forests gave rise to many evils, and *chapters 44, 47, and 48* address themselves to the correction of these abuses.

TOWNS AND TRADE. The England of the thirteenth century was fast emerging from a feudal economy and evolving as a mercantile nation. Magna Carta, though doubtless not by the barons' design, served to promote this development, and several of the Charter's chapters deal with towns and trade. To London, as well as to all other cities, boroughs, towns, and ports, *chapter 13* guarantees all their ancient "liberties and free customs." This, together with John's grant to London five weeks earlier of the right to elect its mayor annually, was an important step forward on the road to a strong and viable system of local government. The appreciation of local government, thus reflected in Magna Carta, so flourished thereafter that soon after English colonies were firmly planted in the New World the colonists created units of local government. Their lives centered about these communities, which survive to this day.

Obstacles to the free flow of trade are removed by *chapters 33, 41, and 42.* In the thirteenth century, rivers were the avenues of commerce, and chapter 33 requires the removal of fishweirs "throughout England." Chapter 41 gives all merchants, of whatever nationality, "safe conduct to go and come out of and into England" and to stay and travel in England, free of illegal exactions. Chapter 42, in liberal terms, says that in time of peace all except prisoners and outlaws may freely leave the kingdom and return. Modern readers, remembering Article I, Section 8, of the American Constitution, will be especially interested to read *chapter 35,* which establishes standard weights and measures throughout the kingdom.

DEBTS AND ESTATES. To deal with the problem of debts owed the Crown (and in those days these must have been widespread), *chapter 9* lays down two rules which, interestingly enough, are still basic to modern debtor relationships: the creditor must go against the debtor for the collection of the debt before he can go against the surety, and a surety who has discharged the debt is entitled to satisfaction from the debtor. *Chapter 10* excuses heirs under age from paying interest on debts owed the Jews. *Chapter 11* sees to it that the needs of widows and heirs are provided for notwithstanding outstanding debts. *Chapter 26* governs the payment of debts owed the Crown at a man's death, and *chapter 27* governs the distribution of the property of a man who dies intestate (that is, without a will).

CHURCH AND STATE. Twice in the Charter, in *chapters 1 and 63*, it is declared that "the English Church shall be free." It should not be thought that this states the principle of separation of church and state in the sense intended by the First Amendment to the Constitution of the United States when it forbids Congress to make any law "respecting an establishment of religion." But the declaration in Magna Carta is of great historical importance. It shows, to begin with, that Magna Carta is not concerned solely with secular matters; chapters 1 and 63 are no doubt the product of Archbishop Stephen Langton's role in the negotiations between King John and the barons. Further, the use of the phrase "English Church," in contrast to the language "Holy Church" in earlier charters, is evidence of the sense of a distinctively English Church, a consciousness which became reality in the reign of Henry VIII.

SECURITY FOR THE KEEPING OF THE CHARTER. *Chapter 61* is of interest to modern constitution makers because it represented an effort to set up machinery to enforce the Charter. It is so detailed that it forms about one-ninth of the entire Charter. However, while its length suggests the importance that the drafters attached to the enforcement

machinery, and while writs survive showing the chapter's
use, the means of enforcement were hardly such as the
King would put up with. Chapter 61 provides for the
barons to elect twenty-five of their number to act as
keepers of the liberties granted by the Charter. These
twenty-five barons, the chapter continues, are to be the
judge of whether the King has breached the Charter and,
if no redress is made, they are free to "distrain and distress Us [the Crown] to the utmost of their power, to
wit, by capture of Our castles, lands, and possessions and
by all other possible means . . . ." Distraint was the means
of compulsion regularly used by the courts of the time to
enforce judgments, but when it is the King who is distrained it is difficult to draw the line between distraint
and rebellion—especially when the distrainers are to be
the judge of whether their distraint is legal. A greater
invitation to quarrels between the King and the barons
could hardly be imagined.

GENERAL CLAUSES. In studying the specific provisions
of Magna Carta, one should not overlook the general
language contained at the beginning and end of the Charter. In *chapter 1* it is said that "all the liberties underwritten," that is, the guarantees of the following sixty-
two chapters, are granted to "all the free men of Our
kingdom," and in *chapter 63,* the concluding chapter, this
idea recurs: "that all men in Our kingdom shall have and
hold all the aforesaid liberties, rights, and concessions . . . ." Too much should not be read into the general
language; those who drafted these phrases in chapters 1
and 63 did not think they were making of Magna Carta
a modern, democratic document whose guarantees would
extend to every man in England, no matter how humble.
But these phrases are meaningful. Although historians

may dispute just who was a "free man" in thirteenth-
century England, "free men" (used in chapter 1) ob-
viously was a broader term than "baron"; moreover,
chapter 63 does not even use the limiting word "free."
At any rate, the existence of chapters 1 and 63 is con-
clusive evidence that the benefits of Magna Carta were
not to be restricted to the barons. *Chapter 60* offers ad-
ditional proof: it says that all the customs and liberties
which the King has promised his subjects in Magna Carta
should in turn be observed by them toward their men.
Whatever the motives of the barons may have been in
extending the Charter's guarantees to others, the fact is
that they did do so, and in doing so they set in motion
theories of personal rights that have had repercussions
down through the ages.

MAGNA CARTA'S INFLUENCE

Whatever its limitations, and there were many, Magna
Carta had considerable virtues. It was because of these
that Magna Carta did not die but lived to inspire generations to come. In the first place, the Charter was a
sensible and practical document. Had it been drafted
without regard to the realities of the time, few people
today would ever have heard of Magna Carta. In its
practicality the Great Charter enjoys a quality that has
often characterized English political institutions and that
is frequently praised by foreign observers. It is but a short
step from practicality to moderation, and from moderation to tolerance. Hence it is not farfetched to say that
Magna Carta, for all its medieval trappings, carried in
it, especially in chapter 39, a seed which was to come to
full flower in the Enlightenment.

But the influence of Magna Carta goes deeper than its contents. The very fact that the King was forced to agree to this declaration of rights and liberties set an example that could never be erased. In a later century when Stuart kings, to cloak their tyranny, invoked the doctrine of "Divine Right," men could look back to Magna Carta as a reminder that free men are not obliged to allow themselves to be ground into the dust.

Magna Carta is important, too, because of the doctrines which it launched on the mainstream of western political thought. However unarticulated, there is in the Charter the principle that we today would call the "rule of law." This is the thrust of chapter 39's "law of the land" and of the chapters which guarantee accessible justice, punishments to fit the crime, the appointment of men who know and will keep the law, and freedom from arbitrary acts by both monarch and lesser officials. So basic even to popular discourse are such terms as "due process of law" and "law of the land" that we can readily say that no contribution of Magna Carta surpasses the impetus which it gave to the development and acceptance, within and without England, of the concept of the rule of law.

Magna Carta's power lay, of course, in the symbolism and moral force that it carried for later times, an influence so great that by the seventeenth century the best-read of lawyers traced almost anything that was worthy and good back to the Charter, including trial by jury, habeas corpus, and Parliament's right to control taxation. Had King John lived for many years after the Charter's signing in 1215, it is possible that Magna Carta would not have survived to have such influence, for not long after the signing John importuned Pope Innocent III to

declare the Charter a nullity. Civil war flared, but for-
tunately for the Charter, King John died in October
1216, as a British writer puts it, "by a surfeit of peaches
and new cider."

John's death brought his nine-year-old son, Henry III,
to the throne, and within days after his coronation Henry's supporters, seeing in the Charter a means of win-
ning friends for the new king, had it reissued. At that
time about one-third of the clauses, most of them dealing
with temporary problems, were omitted. A second reissue
took place in 1217, when the forest clauses were severed
and put into separate "Charters of the Forest." A third
reissue occurred in 1225, by which time the name "Magna
Carta" had come into use to distinguish that charter from
the forest charters.

By this time Magna Carta was well on its way to becoming the cornerstone of the English Constitution. Before
the close of the Middle Ages it had been confirmed thirty-
eight times, a fitting tribute to the reverence which Englishmen came to feel for their Great Charter and the
awareness which king after king had of this reverence.
In 1297, with its confirmation by Edward I, Magna
Carta was placed on the statute books of the realm, and
there it remains to this day.

By the end of the fourteenth century, Magna Carta had
established itself as more than simply a venerable statute;
by then it was a fundamental law. In 1368, for example,
a statute of Edward III commanded that the "Great
Charter and the Charter of the Forest be holden and
kept in all Points; and if there be any Statute made to
the contrary, it shall be holden for none." Here we see

King John. (Courtesy of the Library of Congress)

Lincoln Cathedral copy of Magna Carta (1215). One of the four surviving original manuscripts. Greatly reduced.

(Courtesy of the Library of Congress)

The meadow and island at Runnymede, Surrey, where Magna Carta was agreed to by King John. (Courtesy of the British Information Services)

Magna Carta treated as a superstatute, in other words, as a constitution. The declaration that statutes contrary to Magna Carta are null and void carries an obvious similarity to the language of the American Constitution that it and the laws "made in Pursuance thereof" shall be "the supreme Law of the Land" and to the doctrine of judicial review by which Acts of Congress or of State legislatures are held invalid if they are found to conflict with the Constitution.

During Tudor times there was little talk of Magna Carta, for in that vigorous age of expansion at home and abroad, royal power was not used in such a way as to stir general discontent or opposition. But even while many of Magna Carta's constitutional provisions became dormant in the long transition from the feudal era, other of its provisions were accepted as the basic rules of private law. Thus, in the later Middle Ages and the early modern period, "actions on the Great Charter" were regularly recorded in the law reports. Chapter 4 on liability for waste of assets held under wardship became a standard means of compelling guardians to account for their handling of such property. Chapter 18 provided the basis for legal actions concerning inheritance. A lawsuit brought by a widow against her husband's executor in 1314—a century after Runnymede—based her claim on the fact that "it is provided by the Great Charter of the liberties of England that children, after the death of their father, are to have their reasonable share of the goods and chattels which he had on the day of his death."

In the seventeenth century, with the Stuarts on the throne, Magna Carta once again came into its own. In

part because reliance on Magna Carta by private litigants had confirmed its character as fundamental law
and kept it alive and vigorous, the constitutional or public law features of the Charter were asserted and revived
when Parliament challenged the Stuarts. Troubles over
royal taxation without the consent of Parliament arose
during the reign of James I (1603-25) and intensified
upon the accession of Charles I (1625-49). Other grievances mounted, involving arbitrary and illegal detentions,
the quartering of troops in private homes, and the im-
position of martial law. Seeking action to end these
abuses, members of Parliament invoked the ancient name
of Magna Carta. Sir Benjamin Rudyerd spoke the senti-
ment of many:

For my own part, I shall be very glad to see that good,
old decrepit Law of Magna Charta which hath been so
long kept in and lain bed-rid as it were; I shall be glad I
say to see it walk abroad again, with new Vigour and
Lustre . . . : For questionless, it will be a general hearten-
ing to all.

Glowing sentiments were also expressed by Sir Edward
Coke, both on and off the floor of Commons. In his
Second Institute, completed in 1628, Coke said of chapter
40, the King's promise not to sell or deny justice:

As the goldfiner will not out of the dust, threds, or shreds
of gold, let passe the least crum, in respect of the excel-
lency of the metall: so ought not the learned reader to
let passe any syllable of this law, in respect of the ex-
cellency of the matter.

The result of Parliament's deliberations was the Petition of Right, which the historian Macaulay called "the
second Great Charter of the liberties of England." Like
Magna Carta, the Petition of Right was a restraint on

arbitrary government. After reciting the famous language of chapter 39 of Magna Carta and adverting to grievances against the King, the Petition of Right condemned taxation without Parliament's consent, imprisonment of persons without showing cause, quartering of soldiers on the populace, and the misuse of martial law. To Magna Carta and the Petition of Right were added, in 1679, the Habeas Corpus Act, which required prisoners to be brought before the court promptly after the issuance of the writ, and, in 1689, the Bill of Rights.

The Bill of Rights, embodying the Revolution Settlement which ousted James II and brought William and Mary to the throne, represents a historic extension of the liberties of the people and the rule of law in the tradition that goes back to Magna Carta. Among the provisions of the Bill of Rights are those which outlaw suspending or dispensing with the laws, require consent of Parliament before taxes are laid, secure to the people the right to petition for redress of grievances, restrict the maintenance of standing armies, guarantee free elections to Parliament, secure to Members of Parliament free speech, outlaw excessive bails and fines and cruel and unusual punishments, forbid the manipulation of juries, and require frequent Parliaments. Many of these same rights, of course, are found in the Bill of Rights of the American Constitution and in the State Constitutions.

The Act of Settlement of 1701 completed the establishment of a constitutional monarchy in Great Britain by defining the conditions upon which the Crown should be held. Yet Magna Carta remains the cornerstone. *Halsbury's Laws of England* speaks of the "four great statutes or charters by which the rights and liberties of the subject are preserved and acts of tyranny by the Crown or its ministers restrained." *Halsbury's* names as the first of these the Magna Carta; the others are the Petition of Right, the Bill of Rights, and the Act of Settlement.

Magna Carta was early carried to the New World. Sir Edward Coke, who so eulogized Magna Carta, had a major hand in the drafting of the first Virginia Charter, drawn up and sealed in 1606. That charter grants to all who shall dwell in the colonies "all Liberties, Franchises, and Immunities" that they would have if living in England. These were the famous "rights of Englishmen," the foremost of which, as Coke well knew, were the guarantees of Magna Carta. The same assurance of the rights of Englishmen is found in other colonial charters, including those of Massachusetts Bay (1629), Maryland (1632), Connecticut (1662), Rhode Island (1663), Carolina (1663), and Georgia (1732).

The colonists were acutely aware of these rights. The General Assembly of Maryland in 1639 declared that "the Inhabitants of this Province shall have all their rights and liberties according to the great Charter of England." Specific provisions of Magna Carta found their way into colonial legislation. The General Court of Massachusetts in 1641 adopted the Body of Liberties, the first clause of which drew inspiration directly from Magna Carta's guarantee of the "law of the land" by requiring that no man's life, liberty, or property should be taken "unlesse it be by vertue or equitie of some expresse law of the Country waranting the same, established by a generall Court and sufficiently published . . . ." The Body of Liberties was the outgrowth of the need, as John Winthrop put it, for a fundamental law "in resemblance to a Magna Charta" to prevent the colony's magistrates from acting "according to their discretions."

When revolutionary fevers rose in the eighteenth century, it was upon the "rights of Englishmen," among other things, that the colonists rested their cause. The colonists' claims to these rights are expressly set out in, for example, the Declaration of Rights of the Stamp Act Congress (1765) and the Declaration and Resolves of the First Continental Congress (1774). In 1776, when the break with the Mother Country was at hand, Tom Paine in his influential tract *Common Sense* called for the convening of a "continental conference" whose job it would be "to frame a Continental Charter or Charter of the United Colonies (answering to what is called the Magna Charta of England) ... securing freedom and property to all men ...."

Finally, when independence was declared and the American people turned to the task of creating governments for themselves, it is significant that they turned to English models for the statement of the rights for which they were then fighting the English Crown. The Constitution of Virginia of June 12, 1776, included a Bill of Rights which preserved to the people of that State many of the same rights set out in the English Bill of Rights of 1689: frequent elections, free elections, a ban on suspension of the laws, the outlawing of cruel and unusual punishment and excessive bails and fines, and restriction of standing armies. Later, when a Union was formed and a Federal Constitution adopted, one of the initial actions of the First Congress was to propose to the States for

ratification a Bill of Rights, among which were numbered fundamental guarantees of liberty drawn from
the great charters of English liberty. Here, in the Fifth
Amendment, we find a living tribute to the endurance of
the principle of the "law of the land" laid down at Runnymede 576 years earlier: "No person shall . . . be deprived of life, liberty, or property, without due process
of law . . . ."

Magna Carta was born, of course, on English soil. Its most
immediate influence, not surprisingly, has been in countries sharing the legacy of the common law and British
constitutionalism, notably the United States. But ideas so
powerful as those in the Great Charter are not to be cab-
ined within any one legal system. International norms,
especially precepts of human rights developed since
World War II, have a familial resemblance to the tenets of
Magna Carta.

The modern era has seen tyrannies and oppressive
regimes of the most venal sort, Nazism and Communism,
to name but two. Out of the ashes of World War II rose
efforts to nurture the rule of law and respect for human
dignity. Those who gathered at Runnymede in 1215
would certainly recognize the premise of the Universal
Declaration of Human Rights (1948), which declares that
"it is essential, if man is not to be compelled to have
recourse, as a last resort, to rebellion against tyranny and
oppression, that human rights should be protected by the
rule of law." Moreover, those thirteenth-century
Englishmen might well find echoes of Magna Carta in
such provisions of the Universal Declaration as the "right
to an effective remedy" for violations of fundamental
right, the right to a fair hearing by an independent and

impartial tribunal, and the proscription against the arbitrary deprivation of property.

The rule of law always has its enemies. The nations that rejoiced at the defeat of Nazism soon realized that Communism was every bit as inimical to notions like due process and equality before the law as ideologies of the Third Reich. To the extent that Marxist-Leninist doctrines has any place for "law" or "rights," it was to treat law as the instrument of party policy and rights as being benefits conferred or withheld by the state at the party's whim.

The collapse of Communism in the Soviet Union and in its satellite states in Central and Eastern Europe gave new hope to millions of people long denied the fruits of constitutionalism and the rule of law. Country after country, free from tyrannical oppression, turned to the task of building a new order. Just as the barons' resistance to King John produced Magna Carta, so the liberal revolutions in the postcommunist world saw new constitutions being written. So rich is the tradition of the Great Charter, so readily identified with ideas that have taken root far beyond English soil, that one should not be surprised to find in those new constitutions formulas that bear resemblance to the lasting ideals of Magna Carta. Typical of the new charters are the declaration in the Czech Republic's Constitution of that country's being a "law-governed state" and the recognition, in the Slovene Constitution, the Slovenia "is a state governed by the rule of law."

No one would argue that the framers of the Czech or Slovene constitutions consulted the text of Magna Carta before they drafted their own country's new constitutions.

They did not need to do that kind of research. Magna Carta began, at one level, as a bargain between barons and King. Its principles, however, have long since nurtured and reinforced far more universal traditions. Magna Carta belongs to the ages.

THE TEXT OF MAGNA CARTA

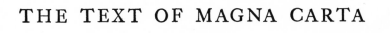

Four originals of the 1215 Charter still exist. Two are to be found where they were originally deposited in the thirteenth century, in the Cathedrals of Lincoln and Salisbury. The other two copies are in the British Museum. The best-known text is that of one of the British Museum copies, Cotton MS. Augustus II. 106. This Cottonian manuscript is the basis for the familiar translation from the Latin found in *Facsimiles of National Manuscripts* (1865), which in turn is followed by W. S. McKechnie in his *Magna Carta* (1914) and in the version issued by Her Majesty's Stationery Office in 1951. The translation that follows, divided into the traditional sixty-three chapters, draws basically, with the courtesy of the Trustees of the British Museum, from the 1951 publication but advances a number of emendations, aimed mostly at achieving readability without sacrificing authenticity. Chapters marked with an asterisk (*) were omitted in the 1216 reissue of the Charter and all later reissues. The number in brackets following each chapter specifies the page in the foregoing commentary at which reference to that chapter may be found.

Scholars have frequently disagreed about the best way to translate into English some of the passages of the Latin original. It is still disputed, for example, whether the Latin "vel" immediately preceding "per legem terrae" ("by the law of the land") in chapter 39 should be rendered as "and" or as "or." There is not space here to discuss these problems. Interested readers should consult more detailed accounts, such as Holt's *Magna Carta*.

JOHN, by the grace of God, King of England, *Preamble*
Lord of Ireland, Duke of Normandy and
Aquitaine, and Count of Anjou: To the Archbishops, Bishops, Abbots, Earls, Barons, Justiciaries, Foresters, Sheriffs, Reeves, Ministers,
and all Bailiffs and others, his faithful subjects, Greeting. Know ye that in the presence of
God, and for the health of Our soul, and the
souls of Our ancestors and heirs, to the honor
of God, and the exaltation of Holy Church,
and amendment of Our kingdom, by the advice
of Our reverend Fathers, Stephen, Archbishop
of Canterbury, Primate of all England, and
Cardinal of the Holy Roman Church; Henry,
Archbishop of Dublin; William of London,
Peter of Winchester, Jocelin of Bath and Glas-
tonbury, Hugh of Lincoln, Walter of Worces-

ter, William of Coventry, and Benedict of Rochester, Bishops; Master Pandulph, the Pope's subdeacon and familiar; Brother Aymeric, Master of the Knights of the Temple in England; and the noble persons, William Marshal, Earl of Pembroke; William, Earl of Salisbury; William, Earl of Warren; William, Earl of Arundel; Alan de Galloway, Constable of Scotland; Warin Fitz-Gerald, Peter Fitz-Herbert, Hubert de Burgh, Seneschal of Poitou, Hugh de Neville, Matthew Fitz-Herbert, Thomas Basset, Alan Basset, Philip Daubeny, Robert de Roppelay, John Marshal, John Fitz-Hugh, and others, Our liegemen:

The English Church shall be free; grant of liberties to free men of the kingdom

1 We have, in the first place, granted to God, and by this Our present Charter confirmed for Us and Our heirs forever—That the English Church shall be free and enjoy her rights in their integrity and her liberties untouched. And that We will this so to be observed appears from the fact that We of Our own free will, before the outbreak of the dissensions between Us and Our barons, granted, confirmed, and procured to be confirmed by Pope Innocent III the freedom of elections, which is considered most important and necessary to the English Church, which Charter We will both keep Ourself and will it to be kept with good faith by Our heirs forever. We have also granted to all the free men of Our kingdom, for Us and Our heirs forever, all the liberties underwritten, to have and to hold to them and their heirs of Us and Our heirs. [pp. 20, 21]

2 If any of Our earls, barons, or others who
hold of Us in chief by knight's service shall
die, and at the time of his death his heir shall
be of full age and owe a relief, he shall have
his inheritance by ancient relief; to wit, the
heir or heirs of an earl of an entire earl's
barony, £100; the heir or heirs of a baron of an
entire barony, £100; the heir or heirs of a
knight of an entire knight's fee, 100s. at the
most; and he that owes less shall give less,
according to the ancient custom of fees. [p. 10]

Reliefs for inheritance

3 If, however, any such heir shall be under
age and in ward, he shall, when he comes of
age, have his inheritance without relief or fine.
[p. 10]

Heir under age

4 The guardian of the land of any heir thus
under age shall take therefrom only reasonable
issues, customs, and services, without destruction or waste of men or property; and if We
shall have committed the wardship of any such
land to the sheriff or any other person answerable to Us for the issues thereof, and he commit destruction or waste, We will take an
amends from him, and the land shall be committed to two lawful and discreet men of that
fee, who shall be answerable for the issues to
Us or to whomsoever We shall have assigned
them. And if We shall give or sell the wardship of any such land to anyone, and he commit
destruction or waste upon it, he shall lose the
wardship, which shall be committed to two
lawful and discreet men of that fee, who shall,

Rights of wards

in like manner, be answerable unto Us as has been aforesaid. [p. 10]

Duties of guardians

5 The guardian, so long as he shall have the custody of the land, shall keep up and maintain the houses, parks, fishponds, pools, mills, and other things pertaining thereto, out of the issues of the same, and shall restore the whole to the heir when he comes of age, stocked with ploughs and tillage, according as the season may require and the issues of the land can reasonably bear. [p. 10]

Marriage of heirs

6 Heirs shall be married without loss of station, and the marriage shall be made known to the heir's nearest of kin before it be contracted. [p. 11]

Rights of widows

7 A widow, after the death of her husband, shall immediately and without difficulty have her marriage portion and inheritance. She shall not give anything for her marriage portion, dower, or inheritance which she and her husband held on the day of his death, and she may remain in her husband's house for forty days after his death, within which time her dower shall be assigned to her. [p. 11]

Remarriage of widows

8 No widow shall be compelled to marry so long as she has a mind to live without a husband, provided, however, that she give security that she will not marry without Our assent, if she holds of Us, or that of the lord of whom she holds, if she holds of another. [p. 11]

9 Neither We nor Our bailiffs shall seize any land or rent for any debt so long as the debtor's chattels are sufficient to discharge the same; nor shall the debtor's sureties be distrained so long as the debtor is able to pay the debt. If the debtor fails to pay, not having the means to pay, then the sureties shall answer the debt, and, if they desire, they shall hold the debtor's lands and rents until they have received satisfaction of the debt which they have paid for him, unless the debtor can show that he has discharged his obligation to them. [p. 19]

Debtors and sureties

*10 If anyone who has borrowed from the Jews any sum of money, great or small, dies before the debt has been paid, the heir shall pay no interest on the debt so long as he remains under age, of whomsoever he may hold. If the debt shall fall into Our hands, We will take only the principal sum named in the bond. [p. 20]

Interest on debts

*11 And if any man dies indebted to the Jews, his wife shall have her dower and pay nothing of that debt; if the deceased leaves children under age, they shall have necessaries provided for them in keeping with the estate of the deceased, and the debt shall be paid out of the residue, saving the service due to the deceased's feudal lords. So shall it be done with regard to debts owed persons other than Jews. [p. 20]

Rights of widows and heirs as against creditors

*No aids
save by
common
counsel*

*12 No scutage or aid shall be imposed in Our kingdom unless by common counsel thereof, except to ransom Our person, make Our eldest son a knight, and once to marry Our eldest daughter, and for these only a reasonable aid shall be levied. So shall it be with regard to aids from the City of London. [p. 11]

*Liberties
of London
and other
towns*

13 The City of London shall have all her ancient liberties and free customs, both by land and water. Moreover, We will and grant that all other cities, boroughs, towns, and ports shall have all their liberties and free customs. [p. 19]

*Calling of
council to
consent to
aids*

*14 For obtaining the common counsel of the kingdom concerning the assessment of aids (other than in the three cases aforesaid) or of scutage, We will cause to be summoned, severally by Our letters, the archbishops, bishops, abbots, earls, and great barons; We will also cause to be summoned, generally, by Our sheriffs and bailiffs, all those who hold lands directly of Us, to meet on a fixed day, but with at least forty days' notice, and at a fixed place. In all letters of such summons We will explain the cause thereof. The summons being thus made, the business shall proceed on the day appointed, according to the advice of those who shall be present, even though not all the persons summoned have come. [p. 11]

*15 We will not in the future grant permission to any man to levy an aid upon his free men, except to ransom his person, make his eldest son a knight, and once to marry his eldest daughter, and on each of these occasions only a reasonable aid shall be levied. [p. 11]

Limit on other lords' aids

16 No man shall be compelled to perform more service for a knight's fee or other free tenement than is due therefrom. [p. 11]

Knight's fee

17 Common Pleas shall not follow Our Court, but shall be held in some certain place. [p. 12]

Justice to be had at a fixed place

18 Recognizances of novel disseisin, mort d'ancestor, and darrein presentment shall be taken only in their proper counties, and in this manner: We or, if We be absent from the realm, Our Chief Justiciary shall send two justiciaries through each county four times a year, and they, together with four knights elected out of each county by the people thereof, shall hold the said assizes in the county court, on the day and in the place where that court meets. [p. 12]

Land disputes to be tried in their counties

19 If the said assizes cannot be held on the day appointed, so many of the knights and freeholders as shall have been present on that day shall remain as will be sufficient for the administration of justice, according as the business to be done be greater or less. [p. 13]

Conclusion of assizes

Fines to be measured by the offense; livelihoods not to be destroyed

20 A free man shall be amerced for a small fault only according to the measure thereof, and for a great crime according to its magnitude, saving his position; and in like manner a merchant saving his trade, and a villein saving his tillage, if they should fall under Our mercy. None of these amercements shall be imposed except by the oath of honest men of the neighborhood. [p. 13]

Same for barons

21 Earls and barons shall be amerced only by their peers, and only in proportion to the measure of the offense. [p. 13]

Same for clergymen

22 No amercement shall be imposed upon a clerk's lay property, except after the manner of the other persons aforesaid, and without regard to the value of his ecclesiastical benefice. [p. 13]

Obligations to build bridges

23 No village or person shall be compelled to build bridges over rivers except those bound by ancient custom and law to do so. [p. 16]

Unauthorized persons not to hold trials

24 No sheriff, constable, coroners, or other of Our bailiffs shall hold pleas of Our Crown. [p. 15]

Ceiling on rents

*25 All counties, hundreds, wapentakes, and tithings (except Our demesne manors) shall remain at the ancient rents, without any increase. [p. 17]

26 If anyone holding a lay fee of Us shall *Debts owed*
die, and the sheriff or Our bailiff show Our *the Crown*
letters patent of summons touching the debt
due to Us from the deceased, it shall be lawful
for such sheriff or bailiff to attach and cata-
logue the chattels of the deceased found in the
lay fee to the value of that debt, as assessed by
lawful men. Nothing shall be removed therefrom until Our whole debt be paid; then the
residue shall be given up to the executors to
carry out the will of the deceased. If there be
no debt due from him to Us, all his chattels
shall remain the property of the deceased, saving to his wife and children their reasonable
shares. [p. 20]

*27 If any free man shall die intestate, his *Intestacy*
chattels shall be distributed by his nearest kin-
folk and friends, under supervision of the
Church, saving to each creditor the debts owed
him by the deceased. [p. 20]

28 No constable or other of Our bailiffs shall *Compensation*
take corn or other chattels of any man without *for taking*
immediate payment, unless the seller volun- *of private*
tarily consents to postponement of payment. *property*
[p. 17]

29 No constable shall compel any knight to *Castle-*
give money in lieu of castle-guard when the *guard*
knight is willing to perform it in person or (if
reasonable cause prevents him from perform-
ing it himself) by some other fit man. Further,
if We lead or send him into military service,

he shall be quit of castle-guard for the time he shall remain in service by Our command. [p. 17]

No taking of horses without consent 30 No sheriff or other of Our bailiffs, or any other man, shall take the horses or carts of any free man for carriage without the owner's consent. [p. 17]

No taking of wood without consent 31 Neither We nor Our bailiffs will take another man's wood for Our castles or for any other purpose without the owner's consent. [p. 17]

Lands of felons 32 We will retain the lands of persons convicted of felony for only a year and a day, after which they shall be restored to the lords of the fees. [p. 12]

Removal of fishweirs 33 All fishweirs shall be entirely removed from the Thames and Medway, and throughout England, except upon the seacoast. [p. 19]

Writ of praecipe 34 The writ called "praecipe" shall not in the future issue to anyone respecting any tenement if thereby a free man may not be tried in his lord's court. [p. 16]

Uniform weights and measures 35 There shall be one measure of wine throughout Our kingdom, and one of ale, and one measure of corn, to wit, the London quarter, and one breadth of dyed cloth, russets, and haberjets, to wit, two ells within the selvages. As with measures so shall it also be with weights. [p. 19]

36 Henceforth nothing shall be given or taken for a writ of inquisition upon life or limbs, but it shall be granted gratis and not be denied. [p. 16]

Writs upon life or limbs

37 If anyone holds of Us by fee farm, socage, or burgage, and also holds land of another by knight's service, We will not by reason of that fee farm, socage, or burgage have the wardship of his heir, or the land which belongs to another man's fee; nor will We have the wardship of such fee farm, socage, or burgage unless such fee farm owe knight's service. We will not have the wardship of any man's heir, or the land which he holds of another by knight's service, by reason of any petty serjeanty which he holds of Us by service of rendering Us daggers, arrows, or the like. [p. 11]

Crown wardship

38 In the future no bailiff shall upon his own unsupported accusation put any man to trial without producing credible witnesses to the truth of the accusation. [p. 16]

No man to be put to his trial upon unsupported accusation

39 No free man shall be taken, imprisoned, disseised, outlawed, banished, or in any way destroyed, nor will We proceed against or prosecute him, except by the lawful judgment of his peers and by the law of the land. [p. 14]

Free men guaranteed "law of the land"

40 To no one will We sell, to none will We deny or delay, right or justice. [p. 15]

Guarantee of equal justice

Free movement for merchants

41 All merchants shall have safe conduct to go and come out of and into England, and to stay in and travel through England by land and water for purposes of buying and selling, free of illegal tolls, in accordance with ancient and just customs, except, in time of war, such merchants as are of a country at war with Us. If any such be found in Our dominion at the outbreak of war, they shall be attached, without injury to their persons or goods, until it be known to Us or Our Chief Justiciary how Our merchants are being treated in the country at war with Us, and if Our merchants be safe there, then theirs shall be safe with Us. [p. 19]

Freedom to leave and reenter the kingdom

*42 In the future it shall be lawful (except for a short period in time of war, for the common benefit of the realm) for anyone to leave and return to Our kingdom safely and securely by land and water, saving his fealty to Us. Excepted are those who have been imprisoned or outlawed according to the law of the land, people of the country at war with Us, and merchants, who shall be dealt with as aforesaid. [p. 19]

Escheats

43 If anyone die holding of any escheat, such as the honor of Wallingford, Nottingham, Boulogne, Lancaster, or other escheats which are in Our hands and are baronies, his heir shall not give any relief or do any service to Us other than he would owe to the baron, if such barony had been in the hands of a baron, and We will hold the escheat in the same manner in which the baron held it. [p. 12]

44 Persons dwelling outside the forest need not in the future come before Our justiciaries of the forest in answer to a general summons unless they be impleaded or are sureties for any person or persons attached for breach of forest laws. [p. 18] *Forest laws*

*45 We will appoint as justiciaries, constables, sheriffs, or bailiffs only such men as know the law of the land and will keep it well. [p. 16] *Appointment only of those who know the law*

46 All barons who have founded abbeys, evidenced by charters of English kings or ancient tenure, shall, as is their due, have the wardship of the same when vacant. [p. 12] *Wardship of abbeys*

47 All forests which have been created in Our time shall forthwith be disafforested. So shall it be done with regard to rivers which have been placed in fence in Our time. [p. 18] *Forest boundaries*

*48 All evil customs concerning forests and warrens, foresters and warreners, sheriffs and their officers, or riverbanks and their conservators shall be immediately inquired into in each county by twelve sworn knights of such county, chosen by honest men of that county, and shall within forty days after the inquest be completely and irrevocably abolished, provided always that the matter shall have been previously brought to Our knowledge, or that of Our Chief Justiciary if We Ourself shall not be in England. [p. 18] *Evil forest customs*

Return of
hostages

*49 We will immediately return all hostages and charters delivered to Us by Englishmen as security for the peace or for the performance of loyal service. [p. 18]

Ouster of
Poitevin
favorites

*50 We will entirely remove from their baili-wicks the kinsmen of Gerard de Athyes, so that henceforth they shall hold no bailiwick in England: Engelard de Cigogné, Peter, Guy, and Andrew de Chanceaux, Guy de Cigogné, Geoffrey de Martigny and his brothers, Philip Mark and his brothers, and Geoffrey his nephew, and all their followers. [p. 18]

Banishment
of mercen-
aries

*51 As soon as peace is restored, We will banish from Our kingdom all foreign knights, bowmen, attendants, and mercenaries, who have come with horses and arms, to the king-dom's hurt. [p. 18]

Restoration
of lands
and rights

*52 If anyone has been disseised or deprived by Us, without the legal judgment of his peers, of lands, castles, liberties, or rights, We will immediately restore the same, and if any dis-pute shall arise thereupon, the matter shall be decided by judgment of the twenty-five barons mentioned below in the clause for securing the peace. With regard to all those things, however, of which any man was disseised or deprived, without the legal judgment of his peers, by King Henry Our Father or Our Brother King Richard, and which remain in Our hands or are held by others under Our warranty, We shall have respite during the term commonly allowed to the Crusaders, except as to those matters on which a plea had arisen, or an inquisition had been taken by Our command, prior to Our taking the Cross. Immediately after Our return from Our pilgrimage, or if by chance We should remain behind from it, We will at once do full justice. [p. 18]

*53 Likewise, We shall have the same respite in rendering justice with respect to the disafforestation or retention of those forests which Henry Our Father or Richard Our Brother afforested, and to wardships of lands belonging to another's fee, which We hitherto have held by reason of the fee which some person has held of Us by knight's service, and to abbeys founded in another's fee than Our own, whereto the lord of that fee asserts his right. When We return from Our pilgrimage, or if We remain behind from it, We will forthwith do full justice to the complainants in these matters. [p. 18]

Respite during Crusade

54 No one shall be arrested or imprisoned upon a woman's appeal for the death of any person other than her husband. [p. 16]

Women's appeals

*55 All fines unjustly and unlawfully given to Us, and all amercements levied unjustly and against the law of the land, shall be entirely remitted or the matter settled by judgment of the twenty-five barons of whom mention is made below in the clause for securing the peace, or the majority of them, together with the

Remission of unlawful fines

aforesaid Stephen, Archbishop of Canterbury, if he himself can be present, and any others whom he may wish to bring with him for the purpose; if he cannot be present, the business shall nevertheless proceed without him. If any one or more of the said twenty-five barons be interested in a suit of this kind, he or they shall be set aside, as to this particular judgment, and another or others, elected and sworn by the rest of the said barons for this occasion only, be substituted in his or their stead. [p. 18]

Restoration of Welsh rights

56 If We have disseised or deprived the Welsh of lands, liberties, or other things, without legal judgment of their peers, in England or Wales, they shall immediately be restored to them, and if a dispute shall arise thereon, the question shall be determined in the Marches by judgment of their peers according to the law of England as to English tenements, the law of Wales as to Welsh tenements, and the law of the Marches as to tenements in the Marches. The same shall the Welsh do to Us and Ours. [p. 18]

Respite during Crusade

*57 But with regard to all those things of which any Welshman was disseised or deprived, without legal judgment of his peers, by King Henry Our Father or Our Brother King Richard, and which We hold in Our hands or others hold under Our warranty, We shall have respite during the term commonly allowed to the Crusaders, except as to those matters whereon a suit had arisen or an inquisition had been

taken by Our command prior to Our taking the
Cross. Immediately after Our return from Our
pilgrimage, or if by chance We should remain
behind from it, We will do full justice according to the laws of the Welsh and the aforesaid
regions. [p. 18]

*58 We will immediately return the son of   *Return of
Llywelyn, all the Welsh hostages, and the chart- *Welsh*
ers which were delivered to Us as security for   *hostages*
the peace. [p. 18]

*59 With regard to the return of the sisters   *Rights of*
and hostages of Alexander, King of the Scots,   *Alexander,*
and of his liberties and rights, We will do the   *King of*
same as We would with regard to Our other   *Scots*
barons of England, unless it should appear by
the charters which We hold of William his
father, late King of the Scots, that it ought to
be otherwise; this shall be determined by judgment of his peers in Our court. [p. 18]

60 All the customs and liberties aforesaid,   *Liberties*
which We have granted to be enjoyed, as far   *to be*
as in Us lies, by Our people throughout Our   *granted to*
kingdom, let all Our subjects, whether clerks   *lesser*
or laymen, observe, as far as in them lies, to-   *tenants*
ward their dependents. [p. 22]

*61 Whereas We, for the honor of God and   *Committee of*
the amendment of Our realm, and in order the   *twenty-five barons*
better to allay the discord arisen between Us   *to enforce*
and Our barons, have granted all these things   *Charter*
aforesaid, We, willing that they be forever enjoyed wholly and in lasting strength, do give

and grant to Our subjects the following security, to wit, that the barons shall elect any
twenty-five barons of the kingdom at will, who
shall, with their utmost power, keep, hold, and
cause to be kept the peace and liberties which
We have granted unto them and by this Our
present Charter have confirmed, so that if We,
Our Justiciary, bailiffs, or any of Our ministers
offend in any respect against any man, or shall
transgress any of these articles of peace or security, and the offense be brought before four
of the said twenty-five barons, those four barons shall come before Us, or Our Chief Justiciary if We are out of the kingdom, declaring
the offense, and shall demand speedy amends
for the same. If We or, in case of Our being
out of the kingdom, Our Chief Justiciary fail
to afford redress within the space of forty days
from the time the case was brought before Us
or, in the event of Our having been out of the
kingdom, Our Chief Justiciary, the aforesaid
four barons shall refer the matter to the rest
of the twenty-five barons, who, together with
the commonalty of the whole country, shall
distrain and distress Us to the utmost of their
power, to wit, by capture of Our castles, lands,
and possessions and by all other possible means,
until compensation be made according to their
decision, saving Our person and that of Our
Queen and children; as soon as redress has been
had, they shall return to their former allegiance. Anyone in the kingdom may take oath
that, for the accomplishment of all the afore-

said matters, he will obey the orders of the said
twenty-five barons and distress Us to the utmost of his power; and We give public and free
leave to everyone wishing to take such oath to
do so, and to none will we deny the same. Moreover, all such of Our subjects who shall not of
their own free will and accord agree to swear
to the said twenty-five barons, to distrain and
distress Us together with them, We will compel to do so by Our command in the manner
aforesaid. If any one of the twenty-five barons
shall die or leave the country or be in any way
hindered from executing the said office, the rest
of the said twenty-five barons shall choose
another in his stead, at their discretion, who
shall be sworn in like manner as the others. In
all cases which are referred to the said twenty-
five barons to execute, and in which a difference
shall arise among them, supposing them all to
be present, or in which not all who have been
summoned are willing or able to appear, the
verdict of the majority shall be considered as
firm and binding as if the whole number should
have been of one mind. The aforesaid twenty-
five shall swear to keep faithfully all the aforesaid articles and, to the best of their power, to
cause them to be kept by others. We will not
procure, either by Ourself or any other, anything from any man whereby any of these concessions or liberties may be revoked or abated.
If any such procurement be made, let it be null
and void; it shall never be made use of either
by Us or by any other. [p. 20]

Pardon of
ill-will and
trespasses

*62 We have also wholly remitted and pardoned all ill-will, wrath, and malice which has arisen between Us and Our subjects, both clergy and laymen, during the disputes, to and with all men. Moreover, We have fully remitted and, as far as in Us lies, wholly pardoned to and with all, clergy and laymen, all trespasses made in consequence of the said disputes from Easter in the sixteenth year of Our reign till the restoration of peace. Over and above this, We have caused to be made in their behalf letters patent by testimony of Stephen, Archbishop of Canterbury, Henry, Archbishop of Dublin, the Bishops above-mentioned, and Master Pandulph, for the security and concessions aforesaid. [p. 18]

Oath to
observe rights
of Church
and people

*63 Wherefore We will, and firmly charge, that the English Church shall be free, and that all men in Our kingdom shall have and hold all the aforesaid liberties, rights, and concessions, well and peaceably, freely, quietly, fully, and wholly, to them and their heirs, of Us and Our heirs, in all things and places forever, as is aforesaid. It is moveover sworn, as well on Our part as on the part of the barons, that all these matters aforesaid shall be kept in good faith and without deceit. Witness the above-named and many others. Given by Our hand in the meadow which is called Runnymede, between Windsor and Staines, on the fifteenth day of June in the seventeenth year of Our reign. [pp. 20, 21]

BIBLIOGRAPHICAL NOTE

BIBLIOGRAPHICAL NOTE

The most authoritative account of the events of 1215 and of Magna Carta itself is J. C. Holt's *Magna Carta* (2nd ed.; Cambridge University Press, 1992), which places the Charter in the context of the law, politics, and administration of England and Europe in the twelfth and thirteenth centuries. Professor Holt has devoted a lifetime to understanding Magna Carta, and a number of his essays and lectures, delivered during several decades of inquiry, have been collected in J. C. Holt, *Magna Carta and Medieval Government* (London; Hambledon Press, 1985).

No one should write of Magna Carta without acknowledging W. S. McKechnie's *Magna Carta* (Glasgow: Maclehose, 1914; reprinted, New York; Burt Franklin, 1958). Though in need of revision on some points, it still remains a natural work with which to begin serious study of Magna Carta. McKechnie's book contains both the Latin and English versions of the Charter, together with a scholarly commentary on each chapter.

Magna Carta Commemoration Essays, edited by H. E. Malden (London: Royal Historical Society, 1917), does not, because of the First World War, contain contributions which had been planned from Continental scholars, but it has an interesting and useful collection of articles by some leading English and American historians of the time, including McKechnie, G. B. Adams, Sir Paul Vinogradoff, and F. M. Powicke. An excellent history of England at the time of the Charter is A. L. Poole's *From Domesday Book to Magna Carta* (2d ed.; Oxford University Press, 1955), a volume in the Oxford History of England. Another useful history of the period is Doris Mary Stenton, *English Society in the Early Middle Ages, 1066–1307* (4th ed.; Harmondsworth, Eng.: Penguin Books, 1965). John Hudson adds to our understanding of Anglo-Norman society in *The Formation of the English Common Law: Law and Society in England from the Norman Conquest to Magna Carta* (London: Longman, 1966). For the constitutional history of the thirteenth century, see J. E. A. Jolliffe's *The Constitutional History of Medieval England* (4th ed.; London: Black, 1961).

For studies of the monarchy, especially that of King John, see Jollifffe's *Angevin Kingship* (2d ed.; London: Black, 1963), Sidney Painter's *The Reign of King John* (Johns Hopkins Press, 1949), J. C. Holt's *King John* (London: The Historical Association, 1963), and W. L. Warren's *King John* (University of California Press, 1978). Also by Holt is *The Northerners* (Oxford University Press, 1961), which concerns the northern barons, the leaders of strife with John.

Turning to Magna Carta's legacy and influence in later centuries, and representing virtually a life's work on Magna Carta, are two books by Faith Thompson: *The First*

Century of Magna Carta (University of Minnesota Press, 1925) and *Magna Carta: Its Role in the Making of the English Constitution, 1300–1629* (University of Minnesota Press, 1948). Ellis Sandoz, ed., *The Roots of Liberty: Magna Carta, Ancient Constitution, and the Anglo-American Tradition of Rule of Law* (University of Missouri Press, 1993), contains, among others, essays on sixteenth-century English legal thought, the age of Coke and Selden, and the seventeenth and eighteenth centuries.

As to Magna Carta's influence in American legal and constitutional development, A. E. Dick Howard, *The Road from Runnymede: Magna Carta and Constitutionalism in America* (University Press of Virginia, 1968), considers the colonial and Revolutionary periods, the state and federal constitutions, and American law after the Revolution, with particular attention to the unfolding of the concept of due process of law.

A. E. DICK HOWARD is White Burkett Miller Professor of Law and Public Affairs at the University of Virginia. He was educated at the University of Richmond, received his law degree from the University of Virginia, and was a Rhodes Scholar at Oxford University, where he read philosophy, politics, and economics. Following his graduation from law school, he served as a law clerk to U.S. Supreme Court Justice Hugo L. Black. He is past president of the Virginia Academy of Laureates, has been twice a fellow of the Woodrow Wilson International Center for Scholars, and has received the University of Virginia's Distinguished Professor Award for excellence in teaching. He has been counsel to the General Assembly of Virginia and a consultant to state and federal bodies, including the U. S. Senate Judiciary Committee. His numerous publications include *Constitution Making in Eastern Europe*, *Commentaries on the Constitution of Virginia*, and *The Road from Runnymede: Magna Carta and Constitutionalism in America*. Often consulted by constitutional drafters in other countries, Professor Howard had compared notes with revisors at work on new constitutions in such places as Brazil, Hong Kong, the Phillipines, Hungary, Czechoslovakia, Poland, Romania, the Russian Republic, Albania, Bosnia, South Africa, and Malawi. In 1994 *Washingtonian* magazine named him "one of the most respected educators in the nation." In 1996 the Union of Czech Lawyers, citing Professor Howard's "promotion of the idea of a civil society in Central Europe," awarded him their Randa Medal—the first time this honor has been conferred on anyone but a Czech citizen.